**Read for a Better World**™

# GOAT KIDS
## A First Look

**ANNA ANDERHAGEN**

GRL Consultant, Diane Craig, Certified Literacy Specialist

Lerner Publications ◆ Minneapolis

# Educator Toolbox

Reading books is a great way for kids to express what they're interested in. Before reading this title, ask the reader these questions:

What do you think this book is about? Look at the cover for clues.

What do you already know about goat kids?

What do you want to learn about goat kids?

## Let's Read Together

Encourage the reader to use the pictures to understand the text.

Point out when the reader successfully sounds out a word.

Praise the reader for recognizing sight words such as *are* and *to*.

# TABLE OF CONTENTS

# Goat Kids

Baby goats are called kids.

Goat kids can stand up and walk when they are born.

Goat kids drink their mom's milk.

Moms call to their goat kids when they go too far away. Goat kids call back.

Why do goat kids stay near their mom?

They sleep by their mom.

Goat kids' eyes help
them see well.
They can see in the dark.

At about two weeks old, goat kids start to eat plants and grass.

They like apples and carrots.

What do you like to eat?

Goat kids like
to climb.
They jump on rocks.

**Where can you jump and climb?**

Goat kids like pets
on the head.

Goats can live for fifteen years or more.

Goat kids jump for fun!

## You Connect!

Have you ever seen a goat kid?

What is something you like about goat kids?

How do you like to play?

## STEM Snapshot

Encourage students to think and ask questions like scientists. Ask the reader:

What is something you learned about goat kids?

What is something you noticed about goat kids in the pictures in this book?

What is something you still don't know about goat kids?

# Photo Glossary

carrot

climb

eyes

plants

# Learn More

Barnes, Rachael. *Baby Goats*. Minneapolis: Bellwether Media, 2023.

Davidson, Rose. *Goats*. Washington, D.C.: National Geographic Kids, 2023.

London, Martha. *Baby Goats*. Minneapolis: Pop!, 2021.

# Index

## Photo Acknowledgments

The images in this book are used with the permission of: © Rita_Kochmarjova/Shutterstock Images, pp. 4–5, 20; © PongMoji/Shutterstock Images, pp. 6–7; © Wirestock Creators/Shutterstock Images, pp. 8–9; © Ginger Design/Shutterstock Images, p. 10; © Nadezhda Bolotina/Shutterstock Images, p. 11; © Nataliia Melnychuk/Shutterstock Images, pp. 12–13, 23 (bottom left); © Ethan Quin/Shutterstock Images, p. 13; © ShotPrime Studio/Shutterstock Images, pp. 14, 23 (bottom right); © GOLFX/Shutterstock Images, pp. 15, 23 (top left); © flysnowfly/Shutterstock Images, pp. 16–17; © schubbel/Shutterstock Images, pp. 16, 23 (top right); © Khorzhevska/Shutterstock Images, p. 18; © Standret/Shutterstock Images, p. 19.

Cover Photograph: © oksana2010/Shutterstock Images

Design Elements: © Mighty Media, Inc.

Lerner Publications Company
An imprint of Lerner Publishing Group, Inc.
241 First Avenue North
Minneapolis, MN 55401 USA

For reading levels and more information, look up this title at www.lernerbooks.com.

Main body text set in Mikado a Medium.
Typeface provided by Hannes von Doehren.

**Library of Congress Cataloging-in-Publication Data**

Names: Anderhagen, Anna, author.
Title: Goat kids : a first look / Anna Anderhagen.
Description: Minneapolis : Lerner Publications, [2025] | Series: Read about baby animals (read for a better world ) | Includes bibliographical references and index. | Audience: Ages 5–8 | Audience: Grades K–1 | Summary: "Did you know that baby goats are called kids? Leveled text and exciting photographs help human kids learn more about playful baby goats"—Provided by publisher.
Identifiers: LCCN 2023033678 (print) | LCCN 2023033679 (ebook) | ISBN 9798765626375 (library binding) | ISBN 9798765629499 (paperback) | ISBN 9798765636640 (epub)
Subjects: LCSH: Goats—Infancy—Juvenile literature.
Classification: LCC SF383.35 .A53 2025  (print) | LCC SF383.35 (ebook) | DDC 636.3/907—dc23/eng/20231108

LC record available at https://lccn.loc.gov/2023033678
LC ebook record available at https://lccn.loc.gov/2023033679

Manufactured in the United States of America
1 – CG – 7/15/24